DADDY'S
girl

MALIKA ROEBUCK

Printed in the United States of America

Keen Vision Publishing, LLC
www.keen-vision.com
ISBN: 978-1-948270-61-8

For every woman who has felt the pain of an absentee father. The cycle of pain ends in these pages.

CONTENTS

INTRODUCTION

What does it mean to be a daddy's girl? We have all heard that term at one point or another, but what does it truly mean? Some think it defines a girl who is extremely privileged by her father and has everything she needs and wants. Others may believe the term describes a girl who is able to get away with any and everything without reprimand or consequence. The truth is, a "daddy's girl" is a female who has been engulfed with the love of a father and has felt the true sentiments of his protection, care, and affection for her. It's something that cannot be compromised or replaced in a girl's heart. Though I never had the privilege of being a daddy's girl, I was able to find that love, protection, care, and affection with my heavenly Father, Jesus Christ.

Fortunately, the basis of this book is not about comparing girls who grew up knowing their natural fathers to those who didn't. Daddy's Girl is a tool intended to help women who haven't quite identified or dealt with the insecurities, challenges, and pain of growing up without knowing their natural fathers. Am I a scholar of this topic? No. Do I have a psychology degree in this field of study? No. However, I do have personal experience in this matter. I can honestly say I have made several mistakes, dealt with low self-esteem issues, and even hated the woman I had become all because I never knew my natural father. Fortunately, I identified those areas so that I could begin the journey of healing.

Ladies, now is the time to identify those issues and attack them head-on. You must be honest with yourself and realize the areas you need to address so that healing and self-growth may begin. I pray my testimony will help you, my sister, identify your areas of hurt and pain, and overcome them.

FACTS ARE STUBBORN, BUT STATISTICS
ARE MORE PLIABLE.

-MARK TWAIN

chapter one

STATISTICALLY SPEAKING

We've heard it all before. One in five, two out of three, one out of every eight, so on and so forth. But what do these ratios actually represent? They are a calculated format often used to explain the likely outcome of a person's situation based on gathered data that shows patterns of similarity amongst others. In short, they are known as statistics. But what are statistics? In my opinion, they are a calculated way to keep track of where we all fit in today's society. So, when you read that one out of every five people in the United States suffers from depression, the ratio suggests that there has been enough tangible evidence reported to support this claim. This doesn't mean someone that is clinically depressed is calling a specific phone number to file a report of their depression to keep these stats current. But, in today's world, there always seems to be a way to document or record just about anything.

Everyone fits into some form of a statistical rating. However, does this mean you need to conform to what the statistics predict about you? Absolutely not! Statistics just let you know where the world sees you in relation to others based on your circumstance. I am a huge advocate of not conforming to the mindset of being just another statistic. From personal experience, I have witnessed people conform based on what society predicts about them. For argument sake, let's say statistics say that one out of every four single mothers is more likely to drop out of college within their first year due to stress and lack of flexibility. One in four single mothers is now expected to drop out of school. Otherwise, the report loses its validity. I also believe this is somewhat psychological. When we read or become aware of a status quo that tries to determine where we 'should' be in life based on our circumstances, in some cases, we subconsciously conform to it. Have you ever heard someone say, "I should just give up. They said I wasn't going to make anything out of my life anyway." or, "Why should I even try? They said it was going to be too hard?" I have, and my response is always, "Who are THEY? And, why are you listening to them anyway?" I've learned, over time, that "THEY" isn't an actual person. For most people, "THEY" is a fabricated being that has become a voice that a person is willing to listen to regarding their potential in life.

If we're not careful, "THEY" has the power to keep us from getting the best out of life. "THEY" can cause us to focus on our misfortune, rather than our opportunities. Listening to anything or anyone that doesn't motivate you in the right direction is a way of conforming to statistical thinking. However, I get that it's hard. I truly do. Sometimes the weight of what we feel is so great that conforming to the negative seems easier than putting forth the effort to push past personal barriers. Statistics say, "Don't try. Just conform to what's already been predetermined for you." I say, "Not so."

All my life, I've heard about my statistic. It should be pretty obvious what that is, right? I was born a fatherless African American girl due to my biological father deciding to abandon me during my infancy. Pretty straight forward. How did that make me a statistic fresh out of the womb? Well, it's simple. I was not the first black girl born into this situation, and I most definitely won't be the last. There have already been reports, data, charts, graphs, you name it set in place to analyze what quality of life a fatherless black girl may experience. So whether I liked it or not, I was born into circumstances that had already predestined my future. Or, so it thought…

I'm aware that the pain of fatherlessness and abandonment is not just limited to African Americans girls. However, it just seems that being a fatherless African American girl comes with its own connotations. At the risk of being politically incorrect, Black, White, or Hispanic -- it doesn't matter. Being a girl abandoned by her father sucks!

Even though I have now grown into a woman, unquestionably, my journey from childhood to womanhood without knowing my biological father was no easy passage.

There were no short cuts, detours, or alternative routes. I had to ride the highway of pain, doubt, and uncertainty for years. According to a statistical report, people like me that have had absentee fathers should be emotionally unstable and distraught for the rest of our lives. I refuse. I can now speak with authority and say that will not be my fate...but it almost was. It took me years to realize what I was doing to myself emotionally before I realized that I had to snap out of the place I was in.

Let's take a second to see what statistics say about fatherless women. Fatherless women are more likely too:

- Lose a certain level of security and protection
- Be uncertain of themselves
- Have low self-esteem, resulting in poor relationship
- choices
- Be the 90 percent that has been found needing to have emotional life savers
- Constantly feel isolation
- Have a high risk of suicide and poverty
- Turn to substance abuse

Do you know what's scary about this? Besides the obvious seriousness of these issues, I've come to realize that these are not just statistics. These problems have been used as coping mechanisms for those who have dealt or are dealing with the pain of fatherlessness. Think about it from this perspective. Have you ever been to the doctor in pain for an issue (cut, scrape, cough, cold, etc.) that just wouldn't subside, and the doctor tells you that it will eventually go away on its own? There's nothing they can prescribe, no antibiotic or medication. It'll just go away in due time. I've been there. Not fun. To be honest, no one wants to hear that their ailment has to heal naturally when they're in pain. In these cases, what do we do? Most of us find alternative ways to cope with pain or discomfort. Why? Well, it's simple. We don't want to deal with the discomfort of the issue. Why wouldn't this be the same mindset for us that have dealt with abandonment? Our minds say, "We must find something to help deal with the pain! There has to be another option or remedy to take away this agony!" This is where the statistical reports come in. For those of us dealing with the pain of not knowing our fathers, there seems to be a bounty of failure on our heads. Statistics say we are more likely (being blunt) to fail. This doesn't mean that we don't have a shot at success in life, we just have so many inner battles that "statistically" there is a slim chance most of us will be able to press past it to reach our true potential.

I can testify that there is hope on the other side of your 'statistical bounty.' Don't allow society to make you feel as if you have to conform to its results. There is nothing wrong or shameful about being a person battling fatherlessness. There is, however, a problem with subjecting yourself to failure due to an unfortunate start at life.

Like some of you, my pain started at the very beginning.

Not physical pain, but mental. I came to realize that whether I liked it or not, dealing with an absentee father was going to come with pain all on its own. As you read this book, you'll see that I experienced my pain in waves throughout my life. One minute I would be completely fine, and the next minute I would feel this overwhelming feeling of shame and guilt that would cause me to mentally succumb to the pain of not knowing my father. Now, just in case you might be thinking I was some sort of a schizophrenic child with unstable moods, I wasn't. (Just to clear the air) I was just a child going through constant cycles of disappointment.

So just like the statistics predicted, I started to do everything that was "statistically expected" of me. I became self-image conscious, which resulted in low self-esteem. I began thinking that everything that was wrong with me came from my father not wanting me. This spiraled into shame and foolishly had me allowing the opinions of others to make me view myself differently. I dealt with isolation for years. I thought that no one around me could relate to my circumstance. I was on my own little island of Patmos. I felt like the modern-day version of John, alone and deserted. Consequently, feeling isolated either makes you feel as if it's better to be alone or it gives you an excuse to put up a wall to 'protect' yourself from others. I chose the wall.

Over the years, I began to take personal inventory over my choices. I would ask myself, "Are you going to stay here?

Or, are you going to grow past this?" Well, I am happy to report that I made the choice not to submit to my pain. I refused to give in and allow pain to rule over my life any further than it already had. I refused and still refuse to be another statistic, and guess what? You don't have to submit to your pain either. You're not a statistic unless you choose to be. Isn't that the beauty in it all? You can choose! You are not bound to the negative status quo. The status quo can be a status no! Sounds clever, but true.

As I wrote this book, I found myself alarmed at some of my struggles. My alarm didn't come from thinking I was too good to go through these types of problems. I was shocked that I allowed myself to suffer for so long. Writing out your problems requires vulnerability, especially when you begin to go down memory lane. "Did I really go through that?" I constantly thought as I wrote. "Wow, I guess I did."

I can candidly say I was ignorant of the things I did to cope with the pain of having a void in my heart. It's almost as if I became skilled at justifying my actions. Everything I did wrong because of my 'daddy issues' had a justifiable excuse and reason. Over time, I learned to stop pointing blame and take ownership of my poor choice to fall prey to statistics. Equally important, I've learned from my struggles. I made a bold choice not to conform to what the world thinks should become of me. This girl, a statistic? Pff. I think not!

BEFORE I FORMED THEE IN THE BELLY, I KNEW THEE.

-JEREMIAH 1:5

chapter two

SEPTEMBER 22, 1987

Like everyone else in the world, I don't remember being born. Nor do I remember making any special requests to God about how I would like to be born. I don't remember picking and choosing which battles to face or what pain I wanted to experience. If I had it my way, I would have chosen the least complicated and painless life available.

Unfortunately, I was born into an unbalanced situation without asking for it, which may explain your life as well. It's like walking into a meeting about you with a room full of people, but you weren't prepped prior to opening the door. Such is life. I don't often reflect on my father not being around when I was born, but more so the love I've had from my family since the beginning. Despite my father's absence, I have been surrounded by an abundance of love and support from my family since day one. In a nutshell… I was a tad spoiled but very blessed. My mom was and still is the most amazing woman to me. It takes a lot to deal with being a single parent and having to raise a child all on your own. What amazes me the most is that my mom knew from the time of her pregnancy that she would be raising me without the help of my biological father. I can't remember the feeling of having two parents from birth because it was never there. My stepfather came into my life when I was around four years old, but before then, it was just my mother and myself all day, every day!

My birthday, September 22, 1987, is the most exciting day of the year for me. Let my family and friends tell it, I treat it as if it's a national holiday! It took me a while, but I started to embrace the day I was born and learned not to feel remorseful or guilty because my father didn't want me to be apart of his life.

Often, children can feel a sense of guilt about their existence once they are old enough to understand that one of their biological parents isn't a part of their lives for one reason or another. Some of those reasons could be an untimely death, drug addiction, too busy working and chasing after their career, or just abandoning their responsibility. Regardless of the reason, no child wants the feeling of a parent being absent during some of their most memorable moments, especially on their birthday. As a kid, when you notice that an essential part of your life is missing, you start to question whether everything is going wrong because you were born.

The first step to my healing process was accepting that God had a purpose in my existence, and more importantly, my biological father left for his own reasons.

19

What am I saying to you? Learn to embrace the day you were born. Realize that your existence on this earth is not a random coincidence. I've heard so many people say to me throughout my life, "He missed out on a great daughter!" Even though I can agree with that statement, September 22nd has become a day that I've learned to always celebrate with gladness even though my father isn't present. I refused to let a day that celebrates my existence on God's green earth to turn into a day of mourning due to someone else's selfish mistake.

Some years were harder than others. During my captivating teenage years, it seemed like every year, around my birthday, I did something that put my mom in a position to exercise her parental card and cancel all of my birthday plans. I mean, all of them! If I had a party planned…canceled! If I had plans to hang out with friends or go to the movies… CANCELED! And yes, I can admit, like most teenagers, I did mess up sometimes. When I look back, I often think, "Sheesh! Was it so bad everything had to be completely canceled, Mom?" I felt like I was traveling, and customs were telling me I couldn't leave the country due to a parking ticket! When my mother implemented a shutdown, it was a shutdown! She did not change her mind.

On one birthday, I remember I had disobeyed her instructions on making a long-distance phone call. To my defense, we had recently moved from New York, and I was extremely homesick! I had just moved away from my cousins and friends and was just starting to come out of that awkward, dorky teenage phase. You know that phase when you're the 'not so popular kid,' but then you start to develop in certain areas of your body *wink wink* and your popularity kicks in? Well, that was me. I was always extremely nice to everyone, most kids liked me, but I was too soft-spoken for the crowd I grew up with. The kids I grew up around had much tougher skin than I did and could defend themselves at the drop of a hat. Me? Not so much. I was a cry baby and easily bullied. So when I started to become tougher as a preteen, I wanted to stick around a little longer to vindicate some of those wrongs committed against me as a kid. All the bullying, mocking, and making me feel like I was a pushover had come to an end. But guess what? We moved! I didn't get a chance to avenge myself before I was swiped away to Maryland. I desperately had to call my cousin to let her know how everything was coming along in my newfound life. Even though I knew better, I figured, "What are the odds of my mom finding out?" Well…. she did find out. That less than ten-minute phone call had enough power to cancel all my birthday plans. My mother got that month's phone bill, saw a long-distance phone call, and put two and two together. She knew she didn't make the phone call, so she knew it was me. I considered blaming my two younger brothers, but they were four and two at the time.

So long birthday plans… nice knowing ya! It was over! I remember thinking, "Did I ask to move? How are you going to rip me away from a place where I grew up and loved and expect me not to phone home?" Needless to say, my little argument meant nothing to her. She gave a directive, and I went against it. So, I ended up laying in my bed and watching Martin for my birthday.

Those moments made me feel like my birthday was cursed. It felt like the day I was born didn't matter to anyone! My mom pretty much shut down my birthday plans like a security breach at Fort Knox. My biological father obviously didn't care due to… well, the obvious. So I questioned my birthday (especially during my teenage years) a lot. I felt unworthy to be born. I felt like Jeremiah, "Cursed be the day wherein I was born: let not the day wherein my mother bare me be blessed." A little over the top, I know, but that's how I felt. I would stay in my room, have pity parties, and imagine running off somewhere to celebrate my birthday the way I wanted to. The year I turned 15, I was so depressed and overwhelmed with 'not being celebrated' that all I did was walk a few laps around the neighborhood. I remember thinking to myself, "If anyone asks me what I'm doing, I'm going to shout, 'IT'S MY BIRTHDAY!' and keep walking." I mean, what can I say? I was a teenager who thought subconsciously that her birthday was hated, so I had to find attention somewhere.

Fast-forwarding to latter years (and not having to fear my mom around my birthday anymore), I grew past the idea that the day I was born is cursed. I am learning every day that every year the Lord allows me to see is just another step into purpose. My reason for being here has nothing to do with those who choose not to be in my life.

Some of you might be in that place I found myself years ago, thinking my birth held no purpose. It just seemed like a day that God picked for me just to be...well, born. My birthday seemed like an annual reminder that 'this man' whomever he is, didn't want anything to do with me.

Isn't it funny how someone else's selfish choice can make you regret your existence? But I say rejoice in the day that you were born! You do have a purpose! God didn't make any mistakes when he created you and I. Even though we were born into the world with a disadvantage (like many others) it's up to us to see the true intent behind God's design. God didn't place any of us here to 'mourn the day' we were born. He gave us life so that we can speak of His goodness assuredly. As for me? I say, let us eat cake and celebrate anyhow!

QUESTIONS ARE A NATURAL WAY OF HEALING AN OPEN ENDED PAST. REMEMBER THAT!

-MALIKA ROEBUCK

chapter three

WHO'S MY DADDY?

As I got older, I began to ask my mother the day-old question, "Who is my daddy?" It didn't require rocket science to figure out that my biological father wasn't around. So, as I began to mature, I asked questions to identify who I was. Do I look like him? What's his name? Has he ever seen me before? Questions like these continued until I felt content enough to move on. Just to circle back and ask even more questions later.

As you develop, you begin to realize how important it is to ask questions. For me, I asked these questions to try to put bits and pieces of him together, find out who he was, and see if it matched with who I was. I believe that no one can truly understand who they are without realizing that there are multi-faceted parts to their roots. What you like, who you are, and your interests and genetic traits can come from both sides of the DNA spectrum. I was and still am grateful that I have a mother who never shunned me and cut me off for asking questions. My mother shared any information she knew about my father to help fill the void in my heart. Relatedly, she dealt with an absentee father growing up, so she was sensitive towards my curiosity. However, being surrounded with so much love, you start to grow out of the questions phase. You begin to just live life and appreciate what you have going on around you. That's exactly what I began to do. I stopped asking questions for a long period of my life because I just wanted to be a kid and enjoy what kids look forward too: enjoying summer trips, cookouts, and spending time with loved ones.

As you can predict, curiosity and questioning found its way to the surface again. We all know how it feels to have everything coasting along just fine, and then, BAM! Something strikes you, and it's back to reality you go. I stopped asking questions about father until I started to feel like something was missing in my life. The 'break' I took from asking a slew of questions was short-lived. My curiosity of knowing "who's my daddy" resurfaced when I was a pre-teen. In my mind, I was owed an explanation about his absence. I guess this was my crazy teenage "I think I'm entitled to know everything" mindset kicking in. I realized that more than likely, I wouldn't ever hear an explanation from him, but my mother could help with at least some of my concerns.

Some say there are always two sides to every story, but I've always believed there are three sides: his side, her side, and God's side. Even though I was not in the business of picking sides, I was grateful to get somewhat of an explanation from one of the parties involved. I was sure that knowing more about him would help me identify who I would grow up to be. Do I eat like him? Do I look like him? Do we share the same sense of style? Are there medical concerns that could impact me genetically? All of these unanswered questions really started to plague me as I got older.

When we are teenagers, our minds begin to wonder a lot! Nothing makes sense to you unless it's broken down into small pieces. If I didn't get what I felt was a thorough enough answer, I went back to my mother again… and again. I couldn't help it! I am grateful that I wasn't overwhelmed by all the information I learned at such a young age. At the core, my questions were my way of trying to understand why he didn't want me as a daughter. Foolishly, I started to wonder if there was something that I could have done to make him stay. Being an emotional teenager was one thing, but being an emotional teenager dealing with prolonged feelings of guilt and abandonment was an entirely different feeling. Can you imagine going through the most complicated years of your life with an identity crisis and feeling like a big piece of you is missing? Well, a lot of us can identify with this feeling, and we also know how uncomfortable and distressing this can be.

Make no mistake about it. There is no crime in asking questions concerning a situation as serious as this one. I mean, think about it… You were an innocent bystander in this situation, so, of course, you have questions concerning the matter. Don't ever feel that you are wrong or even bothersome for trying to put pieces together from a broken puzzle. Questions are a natural way of healing an open-ended past...Remember that! However, know that it is okay if you come to a point where you feel the best thing to do to protect yourself emotionally is to stop asking. You have to find the right emotional balance for you. My encouragement to you? Ask! Ask as many questions as you may feel your heart can handle, but be ready to hear some very revealing truths. For women, it can be scary to open up a can of emotions concerning a man who showed absolutely no interest in having a relationship with you. But you'll learn that running from questions (when you want to know the answer) can be direct avoidance towards healing. Even though there were things I wanted to avoid knowing, my curiosity got the best of me. I felt even worse when I tried to bury my feelings under the pretense of "not caring" because I wasn't being honest with myself. To grow past my inner pain, I had to face the harsh reality that a lot of people in the same situation faced: I had questions, and I needed them answered.

Some of you have had fathers leave you, and questions are the only link to connect you to any inclination of who he is. Some of you may have at least known who he is but didn't have much interaction with him. Some of you have never known what he looked like or spent more than five minutes in his presence. Wherever the cards may fall for you, it doesn't matter. The common denominator is the same: hurt.

Now that I'm over thirty, the question of, "Who is my daddy?" rarely surfaces. The truth is, you get tired of asking the same questions and receiving the same answers. For those of you reading this who are older, you may feel like you've gotten as far as you're going to get. What's the point of wearing my mind out over this, right? And you know what? It's okay! It's okay to be tired. Sometimes, when we're are tired of something or even someone, we make the conscious choice to walk away from the situation to free up some mental space. It doesn't mean that you're a quitter or running from your problems. Only you know when it's time to stop pursuing the situation (no matter what it is) and allow time to do its part. What do we do in the meantime? I believe God designated this time for you to find who you are outside of your disappointment and to examine the battles within yourself.

I PRAISE YOU BECAUSE I AM FEARFULLY AND WONDERFULLY MADE.

-PSALM 139

chapter four

PRETTY DOESN'T CUT IT

Y ou are such a pretty little girl!" I can't tell you how many times I heard this growing up. I'm not conceited; I had a great mom! Like most good moms, she always kept me in the best of the best — from clothes to shoes and even how she styled my hair. My mother took great pride in everything concerning me. I never went without the basics and had more than enough of my wants. Even though I was a tad spoiled, my mother didn't mind snapping me back into reality during my rare ungrateful moments. I was fortunate enough to have a mother raise me with morals, integrity, and respect. Despite not having my father in my life, I was privileged to have a mother who cared for me.

My schoolteachers would often commend my mother on the "outstanding job" she did in keeping me so well-maintained, inwardly and outwardly. At open house during my freshman year of high school, a teacher told my mom how impressed she was when she saw how I dressed for school every day. She mentioned that I was "one of the few girls who dressed ladylike" and how refreshing it was. I guess my teacher was tired of seeing girls come to school half-dressed as if they were headed to a concert as soon as the dismissal bell rang. My mother did a pretty amazing job grooming me into a decent young lady. Also, my mother and stepfather did their best to help me find balance as a child. I traveled, had the privilege of visiting amusement parks every summer, and attended countless birthday parties, sleepovers, and cookouts. To this day, I am eternally grateful for the opportunity I had to enjoy being a child and reaping the benefits of childhood.

Despite all of the grooming and vacations, I still had to face the harsh reality of being a child. Considering the fact that children do not see the beauty in people's indifferences like adults do, I was often teased about my slight overbite, dark chocolate complexion, and skinny physique. "Twig" is one name I often remember hearing growing up because my legs were so skinny they looked like twigs! I was also teased because of my dark skin complexion. To make matters worse, I could tan within five seconds of stepping out into the sun. It was pretty bad for me as a kid sometimes around other kids; I was pretty much punished for my natural features, which were totally out of my control. Kids can be so cruel. There were moments where I felt like God made some sort of mistake with my physical features. "Why are my lips this big and my skin so dark?" "Why do I have to be so skinny that I get teased about it?" All I wanted was to not look like me. I didn't see any beauty in myself and hated, and I do mean hated how I looked.

Now that I am older, I realize that most of my childhood moments consisted of me dealing with a void that I never even knew was there. Being seen as "pretty" to adults and not so appealing to my peers taunted me every day. I think the most devastating part of this was that I genuinely believed if my father had been around, he could have helped me develop a "daddy's girl" mentality, which might have blocked some of the juvenile ignorance I entertained. I was insecure, uncertain of myself, and subconsciously battling my biological father not being present in my life without truly knowing it.

Like me, many children are often born into unfair circumstances. Born with their defenses completely down and unaware of who their parents are and what kind of situation they're being born into. As a little black girl, it was tough enough just trying to live life. Struggling every day with the thoughts of, "why doesn't my father want me?" made matters even worse. I felt like if I had my father to run to, things would have been better. Over time, some deep down twisted part of me thought that he probably agreed with the kids who teased me. After all, he didn't want me. If I wasn't good enough for him to keep, why would I be good enough for him to protect? Oh, the thoughts I wrestled with in my younger years! So many questions, so many doubts, and no clue how to deal with them.

My mother was always present, but my mother is and always will be just one person. My stepfather was a very instrumental part of my life, but he still wasn't my father. So despite having two very loving parents who cared about me, I envied a lot of the girls I grew up with for having relationships with their fathers. It just seemed like they embodied a level of confidence and inner strength I wish I had. They had a bond, a relationship with their dads that I wanted so badly. Just the fact that they had the privilege to say, "Hi Daddy," or "I love you, daddy," stirred up that ugly green-eyed monster inside of me.

I wanted that relationship with a father more than anything on this planet. I often wondered, when will it be my turn to say, "Hi daddy" "What's for dinner, dad" Or, "I love you, daddy" other than when I pretended in the mirror in my bedroom. I grew tired of pretending. I wanted to live the reality of a real father-daughter relationship.

As a little girl and even to this day, I've always had a strong passion for dance. Everything about the expression of dance as an art form has always fascinated me. I guess the ability to convey an emotion or story through your body to a precise rhythm fascinates me!

Luckily for me, my mother was a dance lover also. She LOVED that I had this strong desire to dance because dance was an art that she deeply admired. So, of course, she invested time, money, and more money for me to become the best dancer I could be! Unfortunately, I ran into an experience at my 7th-grade dance recital that almost made me want to forfeit something I was so passionate about.

Everything started fine… I got on the stage, did my two performances, and danced my little heart out as I had never done before! I believed in giving my all on stage, leaving a mark to be remembered by the audience, and that's what I did! Even though I received so many compliments after my performance, shortly afterward, things started to take an emotional turn. Not too long after my group performed, a ballet group of girls around ages six through eight did a ballet performance to the song, "Butterfly Kisses." Just to paint the picture, if you have never heard this song before, I implore you to listen to it when you are extremely happy! Calling this song a tear-jerker would be a serious understatement. It has this soothing, majestic undertone of sappiness that immediately puts you in touch with the most vulnerable parts of you. Apparently, the dance teachers thought a nice touch would be having the fathers dance with their daughters on stage during the performance. As if the song itself wasn't enough to make you cry, now you're watching these young ballerinas flutter around the stage with their fathers like a Disney fairytale. To tie a pretty red ribbon around the dance, the performance ended with the girls on their father's laps as they gazed into each other's eyes. Sigh… Can you imagine the kind of pain that surfaced in my heart watching a performance like that with a father that didn't want me? All of my 'dance mates' were around me crying, feeling the emotions of the performance. I cried too, but for a totally different reason. Pretty? Yea, feeling pretty was the furthest thing I felt at that moment. Jealousy reared its ugly head, and the tears just flowed from my eyes.

Being "a pretty little girl" didn't seem like much to me because I was battling a feeling of hurt that I couldn't shake. As hard as my mother worked to always keep me happy, in those low moments, none of that mattered. I felt as ugly as the jealous monster inside of me. I could tell my mother would try her hardest to compensate for how I felt about not having my father in my life. She would see that hurt, disappointed look on my face, and off to the mall we went for an adventure of retail and Baskin Robbins! Of course, we would talk, but after a while, it all started to sound like the same thing. A lot of women like me growing up have probably felt this feeling before. It's like hitting a really low point emotionally without any understanding of why you feel this way. It's an inconclusive feeling that leaves you wondering, "Why me? Can anyone relate to this feeling?"

The million-dollar question is, "Does being pretty mean anything to someone who's hurting?" Of course not! As I mentioned before, my mother had to work overtime to make me feel beautiful because she knew there was a void in my heart. I've encountered so many beautiful women who seem so broken on the inside. I've also seen women use their beauty to cover up their hurt. I've had to deal with taking off the veil of what I show to society to deal with my hurt. To be honest, growing up, I never felt that I was pretty; I just listened to what people told me because it felt good. I actually felt very ugly because my father was absent from my life. The misconception is that it shouldn't matter who was there for you growing up and that we shouldn't let that impact how we see ourselves. Even though there is some validity in that concept, it doesn't cover all bases.

What some may misunderstand, is that fatherlessness diminishes how you view yourself. Because he wasn't around, I began to see myself as ugly; he wasn't there to affirm me and tell me that I was beautiful to him.

More often than not, people (mostly women) allow life circumstances to diminish the beauty of who they are as a whole person. Many of us suffer from this type of insecurity because we don't know our self-worth. When we feel abandoned or rejected, we begin to see ourselves in a totally different light. So we sometimes look to other men to affirm us in a way that only our fathers truly can. Over the years, I found out that the question I had to ask myself was, "Will I allow my absentee father to predicate my beauty?" I realized that my beauty had nothing to do with him. I didn't need him to be around in order for me to know that I was and still am a beautiful woman of God. Of course, this realization only came as I walked with the Lord, and He began to open up my understanding. Proverbs 31 teaches us that "She perceiveth that her merchandise is good." This reminds us, as women, to know our self-worth and not to allow our validation to fall into someone else's hands. There's a saying that, "Time heals all wounds." From personal experience, I have learned that time does heal all wounds if you use that time to pursue healing intentionally.

As I matured and walked with God, I began to feel better about myself and started to regain my confidence as a young woman. I started to take inventory over my life and realized that a man who didn't have a part in my growing up shouldn't have my validation in his hands.

It is totally normal to wonder, "If my father had been apart of my life, would things be a little different?" However, regain your confidence by encouraging yourself and having the Lord lead you. You're beautiful, you're enough.

SOMETIMES OUR THOUGHTS ARE BACKED WITH SO MUCH INSECURITY THAT THEY CREATE LIES WE BELIEVE.

-UNKNOWN

chapter five

IDENTIFYING INSECURITIES

Have you ever heard someone say that it's best not to make decisions based on emotions? Many people don't realize that emotions are often paired with insecurities. One tends to influence the other. The roots of most of our bad decisions are our insecurities. An insecure person often makes poor decisions in the area where they are feeling the most insecure. So let's focus on this a little… how did I figure out that my insecurities in relationships were due to my father not being around? Unfortunately, I had to learn the hard way. My poor life decisions revealed that to me. I started to notice behavioral traits on my part that were detrimental to maintaining a successful and healthy relationship.

I was first introduced to relationships in my adolescent years. Once my attraction for boys went beyond just wanting to play outside on bikes and roller-skates, my mom knew it was time for a deeper conversation. She helped me to understand the do's and the don'ts' of dating early on. Unfortunately, even with all the guidance I may have received, I didn't listen. I still made poor decisions in most of the relationships I was involved in. Sometimes, as women, we are so broken that we are clueless to what a bad relationship looks or even feels like. Additionally, our insecurities affect our ability to think clearly or recognize that we have insecurities. How do you know if you are battling insecurities? Take a moment to think back to the decisions that you've made. In most cases, the choices you've made and will make reflect the inner battles you may be dealing with or dealt with. Here are a few signs that you may be struggling with some hidden insecurities:

- Compromising your morals
- Constant Guilt and Need for Validation
- Accepting anything and everything
- Unable to leave due to fear of being alone
- Not able to make your own decisions
- Being excessively clingy and attached

In prior relationships, I was very insecure. The men I was involved with took so much from me and offered me nothing in return. Consequently, it was my choice to continue in the relationships knowing what I knew about the person I was dating. In hindsight, I realize I was dealing with an insecure little girl on the inside desperate to know her father. Make no mistake; understanding my cycle of insecurity and brokenness is not something that came to me overnight. This is something I began to realize as I started to become more honest with myself; I wanted to be healed from what I felt but, more importantly, from what I knew I was doing wrong. I felt low, broken, and even dirty sometimes when I would think back to the things I used to accept. But I had to realize the reason why I accepted the things that I did. I had serious daddy issues, and every man I was involved with was an attempt to fill a void.

Most women who have gone through life not knowing their fathers, will, or have, at some point, tried to fill that void with other men. For some, it has become a never-ending search to find male companionship. I was just out of my parent's house when I began to date this guy shortly after being introduced to him by a friend who felt that he would be a nice guy for me to just 'hang out' with. In a very short amount of time, I became intimate with him and found myself in a soul tie situation where I began to want more of his time.

So, the obvious started; I began to do more of the chasing then I should have, and the roles slowly but surely reversed. It's always been understood that women should allow the man to chase them; it's something men have been known to enjoy doing (some of them at least.) However, when those roles start to reverse, most guys start to lose the desire to chase, and often become disinterested. Why? Because it's just in the makeup of men. They are the bounty hunters of love! It gives them a sense of challenge when they can pursue what they want. When that is taken away, often time's interest is lost. This causes some women to use every fiber of their being to re-spark that flame. You start to wonder, "How do I get him to desire me the way he used to?" "How do I get that 'chase' back in my favor?" For most of us that have landed ourselves with some pretty 'bad seeds' of men, the chase never comes back, no matter what we do. So what happens? We begin to compromise our morals (one of the signs of insecurities), and that's precisely what I did.

I began to compromise my morals by starting to accept his lies, poor behavior, and anything else he would do that I knew was unacceptable. There were times we were supposed to spend time, and he would abruptly cancel on me by ignoring all of my phone calls. In one particular instance, we were supposed to go out for dinner and dancing. "Baby, be ready by 7," is what he told me. So like a typical excited "girlfriend," I cut my time short with my family (who lived about 30 minutes away) to get ready for our date. Shortly after I got home, I decided to call him and make sure that we were still on for the evening, but there was no answer. Okay…. no harm, no foul, right? He's probably still working, so I'll give him more time, I thought to myself. I tried to call a second time…. still no answer. By that time, it was half past 6:00, and I still hadn't heard a word from this man. To speed up the story a little, 7 pm comes and goes, 7:30 pm comes and goes, and then it turned into 8:00 pm … still no phone call. Talk about disrespect! I was so disgusted and hurt because this man had the audacity to lie to me as if he had intentions of taking me out, but never did. Do you think that stopped me from continuing to deal with him? Nope. Consequently, due to my need for companionship, I stayed with him despite what happened.

One day, I decided it was best to end our relationship when I caught him in the biggest lie of them all and decided enough was enough. But this story is a prime example of how I was exemplifying "The signs" and not even realizing it. I was utterly blinded by the fact that I was drowning in insecurities because I just saw it as 'wanting companionship,' not realizing that joke of a relationship was far from true companionship. I often look back and ask myself, "What in the world were you thinking? Why didn't you feel that you deserved better? Don't you know your self worth?" But the truth was, I didn't know my worth, and I didn't feel like I deserved better. I felt that he was a man that was showing me interest; I might as well entertain it.

This brings me back to my original point. If a young girl doesn't have a good or even existent relationship with her father, as a young woman, there is no one for her to compare guys too. In most cases, fathers being present help little girls develop into women that set respectful standards for who they will and will not date. This does not mean that women who grew up with 'daddy issues' have no standards and morals and just fall for anything. It just means that most of us are subject to being more vulnerable in our hearts, and later in life, we discover we tried to fill the void (knowingly and unknowingly) with other men. It could almost appear as if there is a certain level of desperation in us because of our desire for male companionship.

VALIDATION

Can we talk about validation for a moment? Every time I hear this word, it reminds me of someone being stamped with a seal of approval. For women battling insecurities, the need for validation is like venom being injected into our self-esteem; it's killing us. Why? Because it can turn into an endless cycle of needing confirmation that you may never find. So what happens? You keep looking for it in all the wrong places. It strips you of your happiness, your time, and your self-esteem. Consider this, when you envision a woman of confidence and virtue, what do you envision? The word of God gives us a road map of what a "Virtuous Woman" looks like. She embodies her identity in Christ; she knows her worth and makes no apologies for it. She walks with integrity and doesn't lower her standards for temporary satisfaction. She occupies her time wisely, taking care of her inner-self because she realizes beauty is vain. Most importantly, she fears the Lord and subjects herself to the will of God. Doesn't sound close to a woman seeking validation, does it? Becoming a virtuous woman doesn't mean that you won't have complicated circumstances. Walking in virtue is a constant effort we as women have to make strides in every day. What is one of the main killers of that stride? I call it the "Lot's Wife Syndrome" of constantly looking back. Looking back for validation, looking back for someone to affirm you.

I know some of you may think, "What about stepfathers?" Just to clarify, there is absolutely nothing wrong with having a stepfather. In most cases, women grow to appreciate the father figures in their lives. However, the absence of the biological father still leaves a lot of unanswered questions. This, by no means, discredits stepfathers who have stepped up to be strong father figures.

My stepfather has been in my life since I was four. Yes, I was fortunate and blessed to grow up with a father figure in my home, but I still felt empty on the inside. Sometimes, being the "stepchild" is harder than having no father at all. You constantly wonder, "What can I call him?" "Is it safe to call him dad and not offend his other children?" You spend so much time contemplating in your mind how to approach the relationship than actually having one. Being so young with a stepfather is already awkward for most kids. If you were anything like me, you tried your hardest to make sure you didn't make any of his other children feel awkward about your relationship with him. With this in mind, there were times I felt that there were emotional disconnects between my stepfather and me, mainly because I knew he wasn't biologically connected to me. From day one, my stepfather has done so much for me physically and financially that it would be challenging for me to confine it all into a few sentences. I'm grateful and always will be. However, as a child, his love for me didn't overshadow the fact that there was no biological connection. For a while,

I allowed that thought to consume me, and I cried for a daddy to call my own.

While I don't believe that my bad choices are his fault, I do believe his influence would have guided me in a better direction of decision-making. Women make better emotional choices when their father has been around to guide them. As I matured, I learned to stop blaming my father's absence and get to the root of my poor choices. I implore you to do the same. Take the time to reflect on the parts you played in your decision-making. Why? Well, it's called accountability. You won't find your healing until you begin to take ownership and face your truth. Be willing to be honest and transparent with yourself. Take a look at the patterns in your decision making. As you confront all these awkward, vulnerable feelings, don't be ashamed! A part of growing is identifying weak areas so that you can move past it. Being vulnerable allows you to address issues before they become too deeply rooted.

Being vulnerable was one of the most challenging parts of writing this book; I had to be open and willing to admit my mistakes. I don't know of anyone who wants to remain a victim of their hurts and not grow and heal past it. I was led to write this book to show that there's no shame in what may have affected us in the past and that all pain has a root and a cause. You are going to get past the hurt and pain you feel. Identifying insecurities is just a beginning path towards healing and growth.

I'M OKAY! MY BIGGEST LIE...

-ANONYMOUS

chapter six

I'M OKAY!

To this day, I still find humor in those video clips or commercials of people severely hurting themselves and then shouting, "I'm okay!" as if nothing happened. I'm sure you've seen the ads where someone falls out of a faulty chair or falls down a flight of stairs and then announces, "I'M OKAY!" as a way of making light of the incident. In addition to declaring, "I'M OKAY!" they would shoo away any sort of help. This is so humorous to me because the severity of what happened makes it clear that the person is NOT OKAY! and they need help.

Outside of good kicks I get out of the commercials, I often wonder what type of message these clips send about being in pain? Yes, in these cases, the depiction of pain advertised is mostly physical, but mental and physical pain share the same amount of mental space. Is the message that when you're severely hurting that you're supposed to save face, not let on to your pain, and lie about your well-being? Is it all a matter of pride? Do we ever really want to admit to others when we are not doing okay? I realize that those commercials and videos are just a sheer form of entertainment, but I believe they hold a deeper meaning.

It's has been said, "There's a lot of truth behind a joke." Often, when someone is deeply hurting, they'd rather not expose their vulnerability for the world to see. Just like those funny videos, they'd rather keep the "I'M OKAY" mentality than confessing their pain. Now, in this day and age, I totally understand what it means to keep private matters private. On the other hand, it's healthy to understand that sometimes, you're just not OKAY, and that's fine too! Over the past couple of years, I've realized that my non-existent relationship with my father hurt so deep that I developed the "I'M OKAY" mentality without even realizing it. How do I know?

As I mentioned in previous chapters, I've done a lot of heart work to get where I am now. This included a lot of time self-reflecting on past decisions, my way of thinking, and how I processed past hurts and disappointments. I'm not sure when it happened, but somewhere along the way, as a child, I developed the "I'M OKAY" mentality. Remember how I mentioned that when people asked me how I felt not knowing my father, I'd respond, "I'm fine"? As a child, the seriousness of the matter hadn't settled in my mind yet. My maturity and understanding of abandonment hadn't quite taken root. Yes, I dealt with a lot of discomfort due to not knowing my father, but certain matters become more serious over time. Like most children, you only care about what your condition of life is at that time. Some children experience hurt very early in life and feel everything from an early age; however, this wasn't the case for me. I had questions and often brought my concerns to my mother, but after she addressed whatever I was asking, I left the subject alone until I felt it was time to ask again.

Most of you reading this book can agree that you are NOT OKAY. You may have experienced some level of pain growing up as it pertains to your relationship with your father. But you know what? THAT'S OKAY! Sounds weird, right? How can it possibly be "OKAY" that you have are dealing with hurt from your father? I say It's OKAY because you're at a place where you're confronting your true feelings, and that's the best thing you can do on your road to recovery.

WE'RE SO MUCH ALIKE

I'll never forget the moment I got "the call." It was Christmas, and I was at work, doing an overtime shift. I absolutely hated the fact that I had to work on Christmas, but unfortunately, I wasn't one of the people who could opt out of working. During my shift, I abruptly got a text message from my mother telling me to call her immediately. Since I am a concerned daughter, I jumped up from my desk and took an impromptu 15 minute break to call her.

"Malika!" she says.

"What's going on, Ma," I responded quickly.

"You will never guess who I found on Facebook today,"

she said nervously.

"Who?" I asked.

"Your father!" She exclaimed. I was silent. "Malika, you still there?"

"Yes, I'm still here," I said. It's like I could hear the words she was saying, but couldn't process them. My mother was basically telling me that the man known as my father had been found. After 25 long years.

Once my biological father 'appeared' back into my life (strong emphasis on appeared) by way of social media, I felt a rush of so many emotions at once. After taking a few days to deal with my feelings, I realized that I was truly NOT OKAY. After all these years, everything I never truly felt hit me intensely all at once like a head-on collision. Although I've mentioned time and time again how I've dealt with a roller coaster of emotions growing up, that's all they were... emotions. The pain of the situation hadn't surfaced until the time I was introduced to him on Facebook.

As weird as this may sound, even though I was starting to feel comfortable with him not being in my life, I still had this small ounce of hope that things would reconcile between us.

I needed to confront my anger, vulnerability, and hurt! Unlike those commercials, I couldn't say I was OKAY. It was too far from the truth. I couldn't believe I was about to actually look at a picture of a man who I knew nothing about except his abandonment issues. I often told people that I could have stood next to my father in a grocery store and wouldn't have known who he was. Needless to say, after three days of stalling to look at his picture, I finally saw a reflection of myself that I've never seen. I was finally able to see the man known as my father that I couldn't even pick out of a lineup if I had too. The first thing I said when I looked at the photo was, "Wow, I look just like him!" But how dare I say that, right? Why would I want to share my looks with a man that obviously didn't want anything to do with me? But again… this is a part of being honest with myself.

Denying how much we looked alike would have just been me hiding behind my true feelings. One thing I appreciate about social media, especially Facebook, is that it shows a little bit of every area of your life; unless you choose to block it. From pictures alone, one can draw a conclusion on the type of person you might be. The second thing I noticed as I looked at his profile was his likes and dislikes as far as foods, movies, etc. Once again, I saw another similarity that we shared.

Let me just pause here to be clear … by no means was I happy about any of this! I wasn't basking in the ambiance of seeing my father for the first time and daydreaming about our shared likes/dislikes or similar tastes in movies… I was hurting! I was hurting because I had to find the courage to want to know more about this man. It wasn't easy for me to see his pictures, what he liked to do, or where he liked to go. It was just another reminder of how he went on through life without me. As I scrolled through his Malika-less life, I started thinking back to when he abandoned my mother and me and felt enraged. "How dare you even have a life! Must feel good to go through life without a care in the world about your responsibility!" I said to myself.

Want to hear the irony of all this? The more I learned about him, the more I realized that he was also dealing with the "I'M OKAY" mentality. He went on with life, not caring about his responsibility, aka me. In his mind, I wasn't his because he never had the courage to confirm his paternity before he decided to cut ties with my mother. So, it's quite evident that at some point in his life, he developed the same mindset that I did. I was OKAY not knowing him just like he was OKAY not knowing the truth about me—willful ignorance.

IS THAT YOUR "REAL FATHER?"

Growing up in New York, I lived in a typical middle-class neighborhood with plenty of single-family homes filled with the 'typical' American family; biological father, biological mother, and children all in the same household. What I remember most is spending a lot of time outside playing with kids that appeared to be just as "normal" as me. "Normal" meaning that they too may come from a home with a blended family like mine with a stepfather instead of a biological one. However, the advantage almost all of them had over me was that they at least knew their other biological parent. For me, it was just a cold, flat out abandonment; they at least had some sort of distant relationship with their missing biological parent. They may spend weekends with their mother or father or spend the holidays. Unfortunately, I couldn't even say that much. I had no trace at all to my paternal side.

However, as a child, I didn't dwell on that too much. All I cared about was playing outside right after school and making sure all my buddies were ready to ride bikes and play 'Ding, Dong, Ditch.' However, as most people know, kids are very observant and would ask me questions about why I never called (who they knew to be my father), "Dad." To be honest, there's no long drawn explanation as to why. I just didn't. I never called my stepfather 'Dad' because I felt awkward about doing so. He never made me feel like I couldn't, but it just wasn't something that was imparted on me by my mother to do.

So, when I was asked this question, you can imagine how much I hated it. Being asked the million-dollar question of, "Is he your real father?" used to make me want to bury myself in dirt and hide. I think it was the feeling of knowing that I had a laundry list of questions coming after I would say no. What has always fascinated me is that even back then, kids knew the difference between a father and a REAL father. I knew that saying no would lead to more questions like, "So, he's not your real father? What happened to your real father? Where is your real father? Why are you not with your real father?" The conversation would eventually lead to me going into detail about my entire family. Just saying, "Oh...he's my stepfather" wasn't enough for most of those kids. Looking back on it, I think this was the time when I felt the most vulnerable. As a child, you feel like you must answer everyone around you, even about circumstances outside of your control. So whenever these sudden questions arose, I would feel nervous energy in the pit of my stomach. I was nervous, thinking whether or not my friends would consider my circumstance weird or 'not normal' because I didn't know about my biological father. Even though some of them could connect to my situation, where we disconnected is the fact that they at least know or have known their biological side.

As annoying and redundant as it was, I always seemed to cave in and answer all the random, awkward questions about my father. This was when I remembered I would start to feel that feeling of abandonment and insecurity. It was one thing to battle your inner thoughts and deal with your issues privately. However, it's another to openly speak about a situation that makes you uncomfortable. I would start to think to myself, "Why did he leave? Why do my other friends have both of their biological parents, and I don't?" Shamefully to admit, I would sometimes fabricate stories to my new "gullible" friends (when we would move, which was often) about how my father was out of town on business or in the military. But after I lied, I would feel incredibly low because I knew the truth would someday come to light.

Even at a young age, I was very much afraid of starting to feel ashamed that I was a part of a blended family. Now, I absolutely love blended families! To me, it shows how God is able to blend two people together from multi-faceted backgrounds and beliefs and give them the tools they need to make their families work under the same household. But as a child, coming from a blended family warrants a lot of questions from other kids and even judgment.

I realize now that I was using the "I'm OKAY!" tactic because I wanted to protect myself; I mean, what child wants to walk around feeling like they are different from their peers? As a child, fitting in with those around you meant everything! So in our childhoods, we were more prone to protect our image than we may have realized. I can't ever recall a time where I confided my true feelings to a classmate or childhood friend about not knowing my biological father. I automatically assumed that no one could identify with what I was feeling.

Can you relate? Did you ever feel like this growing up? If so, after reading my story, you can see that you definitely were not alone! People often place a strong emphasis on how hard things are for adults (which they indeed are), but oftentimes, we don't consider how challenging life can be for children, especially ones with challenging beginnings. As I mentioned in an earlier chapter, I never went without anything growing up; I had everything I needed, including love, support, and protection. So from others' perspectives that have dealt with terrible tragedies growing up, a little black girl growing up in New York without her father doesn't seem all that bad. But trust me, it is.

So now that we examined what it was like for me as a child and I'm pretty sure you've taken a trip down memory lane too… What can be done to overcome this? How do we brush aside those vulnerable memories from our childhood when we were embarrassed about things we couldn't explain? Are you prepared for this answer? We don't.

The key isn't to brush your feelings aside, but rather use it as fuel in realizing that everything you've felt was perfectly normal. No one can relive your life for you. No one can tell you to just 'Get over' something that they may not even be able to relate too. Don't be that person that feels the best way to heal what you've been through is to try to forget it. This is how the "I'm OKAY" mindset begins to set in. You begin to use this tactic to cope with your true feelings as opposed to just saying, "You know what? My childhood actually did have some sucky moments, but that's all right! They were MY MOMENTS!" Not everyone can relate to my story, but it doesn't make it less real. All we can do is confront our truths so that we can continue to walk in our deliverance as strong women as opposed to broken little girls.

After a while, I started to develop the 'Who Cares' state of mind because it's really not my battle to fight. A lot of us growing up have faced a lot of unfortunate circumstances that have made us feel ashamed or embarrassed. But I've learned that despite what I've been through, I'm not a victim of my circumstance. You may be wondering if I still battled with the "I'm OKAY!" mentality beyond childhood.

To be honest, yes. There were times in which "I'm OKAY" was my response to the questions that were asked. I'd rather not deal with the pain, so I'd hide behind it. But then I began to realize that this wasn't a healthy way of dealing with the pain in my heart. I began to realize that the same mindset I had as a child could follow me even into adulthood if I didn't deal with it.

FORGIVENESS & FEAR

Coming into my adult age and having the mental capacity to really take it all in, the battle that I began to face was realizing the betrayal of my father leaving my mother and me defenseless. It was if the scales fell from my eyes, and I could see the situation for what it truly was. I started to look up towards God and ask Him, "Are you even dealing with his heart about this?" I couldn't deny that I had and still have questions that I can only get from the Lord about this situation. So I've spent a lot of my time on my knees praying about it and asking God to give me clarity on whether or not this situation will ever be exposed.

Some years ago, when my mother first found him, the Lord and I had a VERY long conversation about forgiveness and fear. The Lord began to deal with me and tell me that I had to forgive him for his transgression because it's not my place to hold anything against his charge. My place is to forgive him and be in a position to hear what he has to say if ever I got an opportunity to meet him.

This was extremely hard for me to grasp because I felt

like I had every reason in the world to hold this act of sin against him. But I had to consider that forgiveness towards others is how God forgives us. To further this point, Matthew 6:14-15 states, "For if you forgive other people when they sin against you, your heavenly Father will also forgive you. But if you do not forgive others their sins, your Father will not forgive your sins." Okay, Lord, I hear you! At that point, I had a decision to make on forgiving him (which we'll discuss more in a later chapter). Secondly, the Lord also wanted me to confront fear because there was a task at hand he wanted me to fulfill. Within two weeks of me just simply seeing a picture of my father on Facebook, the Lord instructed me to utilize social media to send him a letter. The letter I was instructed to send to him wasn't to bash him or be confrontational, but rather to introduce myself to him and offer him the opportunity to reconcile a long lost relationship. Do you want to hear the part that sucks? The Lord never told me when or if I would get a response. According to my count, I sent that letter in 2013. At the time I released this book, that was seven years ago. At this point, you can pretty much imagine that I have all kinds of questions about why God had me to do that. But whenever I begin to question why I even sent him that letter or was if it was all in vain, the Lord reassures me that it will all make sense "one day." Until that day, I've tried to keep my focus on maintaining my faith that the Lord will make good on His promise.

ACCEPTANCE

Have I mentioned yet that there is a pivotal point to the "I'm OKAY!" mentality? No? Okay, well, here it is: The main thing I want you to remember about this is that you can actually change this frame of mind from a concept of basically...denial to a means of acceptance. What do I mean by acceptance? YOU have the power to accept that things may never change between you and your father. If any of you are like me, I'm still waiting for God to manifest his promise. As I mentioned earlier, I don't know when God is going to allow a relationship between my biological father and me to happen, but I have to hold onto my faith. For some of us, faith is all we have at this point.

No matter which short end of the stick you've been handed, always keep in mind that you have the power to change the fate of how you grow from it. Be honest with how you feel and defeat the "I'm OKAY!" state of mind. Making excuses nor denial are healthy ways to heal from pain and disappointment. It's OKAY to admit that you're NOT OKAY! It's OKAY to cry and feel vulnerable about your past. Develop the mindset that you can be free, and you will be on your way to self-freedom! THERE IS NOTHING LIKE IT!

ONLY GOD CAN FILL OUR VOID.

-LAILAH GIFTY AKITA

chapter seven

REPLACEABLE

The rule of thumb, for most people, is…. if you ever lose something, replace it. Why? Because depending upon what it is, we simply don't want to do without it. Instead of coping with losing it, it's best to go out and find a replacement of the exact same thing or something that mimics it closely. I know I'm guilty of this. I've lost sunshades, shoes, and my all-time favorite, gloves! But no matter what I've lost, I've always had the mentality that it was easily replaceable. Consequently, for most women, we've applied that exact mentality to our daddy issues. We subconsciously believe, "He didn't want me so someone will." Big mistake.

John, Dante, Eric, William, Richard, Michael, Travis… ugh….The list could go on forever. However, do any of these names look familiar to you? Welp! I want you to meet "The Replacers!" I think you know what I'm talking about. Let's be honest, ladies…. A lot of us have been in some pretty dysfunctional relationships because we were trying to overshadow some deep dark hurt. The worst part is that some of us didn't even know we were doing it for this reason. Am I guilty of it? YES! None of those guys listed were my kryptonite, but you get my drift. Being blatantly honest, I have to say that a good 70% of the men I've dated in my lifetime were "void fillers." It doesn't mean that I didn't enjoy my time with them or that I wasn't trying to pursue the relationships long term, it just meant that I realized (after the fact) there was a deeper root of loneliness I hadn't addressed. It always seemed that I realized AFTER the relationship was over that it was probably best for me to be alone. I really needed some time to evaluate myself. There's only one man in my life that I can say I've dated that I felt like I actually began to grow with as a broken woman, and that's my current husband. God will do it, ladies!

However, let's rewind time to before I met my husband to examine the guys I call "The Replacers." The year was 1943... just kidding! I'm not that old. The years were actually 2007, 2008, and 2009; three years of just back-to-back relationship craziness! I wasn't involved in anything too serious around this time, but this is when I can say I began to feel my absolute lowest. Remember a few chapters back when I talked about this guy I dated who consistently lied to me, but I stuck around? Well, just to give you a feel of how messed up these years were, he was one of the few that I dated during this time. Unfortunately, he wasn't the only one I fell for. Shortly after him, there was another 'John Doe' I dated that was (in my eyes) better than the last guy but still had his share of issues. One of those issues being that he had sneaky tendencies and didn't like to be questioned. So, yes. You guessed it! That relationship didn't last long.

I often think back now and ask myself, "Why didn't you think you deserved better? Didn't you know what you were worth?" To be honest, I didn't know my worth, and I obviously didn't think I deserved better because I kept running into the same circumstances. But not knowing who you are and 'whose' you are can cause a lot of mental uncertainty. A lot of women fall into or have fallen into this mindset at some point. Completely broken on the inside, they're in relationships thinking that a 'temporary boyfriend' will help. This is the furthest thing from the truth. Now, is there anything wrong with dating casually? No, not at all. Sometimes, we just date for fun or companionship. The only person who knows if you're trying to cover a void is you! For a long time, I was in denial about my void fillers. Now, let me be clear. I wasn't stupid! I didn't just fall into any old thing. My downfall was that I knew better and still proceeded to entertain the relationship anyway. So, I guess there was a little pinch of stupid floating around in there somewhere.

YOU ARE THE FATHER

When I was at home for a few months during my unemployment season, I watched daytime court TV shows. I normally liked to watch the civil suits, but sometimes, the paternity court shows would spark my curiosity. One of the main things that began to stick out to me, in some of the cases, was that the judge was able to see right off the bat that most of these women coming into paternity court had deeper rooted issues than just conceiving babies with men. Most of the women would drop hints about what led them to the situations they were in. Over 75 percent of them confessed to not knowing their fathers. I thought about this and realized (as if I already didn't know) there is so much validity behind broken women making poor choices. I didn't know those women on TV, but I could relate so closely to their hurt and insecurities. Thanks be to God that no children were conceived from any of my past relationships, but I can still identify with their hurt. The problem they were facing is that they felt unwanted by their fathers and looked for 'fatherly' love with 'temporary boyfriends.' Consequently, for some, it resulted in an unexpected pregnancy. From situations like this, I stand behind the fact that there are or have been "replacers" in our lives, who have guided us in the wrong direction. I know this to be true because I wanted to replace my father so badly! I figured this would be the best way of eradicating him from my mind and heart. This had to be the biggest recipe for failure.

THIS SEEMS FAMILIAR

In case some of you haven't picked up a theme here, this is not about feeling ashamed. But I did warn you that we would get into the 'Nitty Gritty,' right? How else are we supposed to heal and take hold of our futures? Earlier in the chapter, I wanted to get your brain flowing, so I asked you to recall replacers in your life and how you knew they were indeed a "Replacer." Well, if you've been doing your 'mental homework,' you've probably realized by now why some of those relationships either ended so badly or left you feeling so low. When you go through life with hidden hurts and don't address them, when situations arise similar to the one you're fighting in your heart, it's hard for you to recover from it. This is why you spent so many nights crying. You couldn't grasp hold of your emotions. In our minds, we felt like the world was pretty much ending due to a 'familiar' hurt that we couldn't quite place our fingers on.

For me, when a relationship ended, it took me a very long time (except for one in particular) to recover because my mind could only focus on companionship. That's all I saw, and that's all I wanted. Forget the fact that the person and I couldn't agree on much and always had screaming matches and arguments... at least I had someone, right?

Years back, when I was in a relationship with who we'll call 'John Doe," everything (and I mean everything) was going wrong! Not only were we living in a whirlpool of sin, but we also could not stop fighting each other to save our lives! I'm talking about fights that would often result in me having to stay at someone else's house because neither one of us could control our anger. After a while, I started thinking that maybe he treated me the way he did on purpose. Maybe he thought I couldn't decipher the difference between love and abuse. And when I say abuse, I'm not talking about physically, but more so verbally. Regardless of which form abuse comes, it's still abuse. There were days that I used to foolishly think that our relationship would go on forever. I think that was my, "inability-to pick-a-good-man- ITIS" kicking in. Fortunately, through God's grace, I was not only able to survive the relationship, but I learned a valuable lesson from it. The lesson learned was never to allow my emotions to dilute my common sense. My sense told me that it was a toxic relationship, but my emotions told me to stick it out and see what was next. My curiosity kept me crippled because I was determined to see if things would change.

WHAT IF?

When my Bishop often preaches about fear, he says, "Fear has a way of immobilizing you." As if to say, because you are afraid, fear has now put you in a place where you don't want to take the next step towards help. I believe that curiosity has the same effect on us that fear has. Sometimes, we are so curious about the "What if?" factor that we are fearful of embarking on change. "I want to leave him, but WHAT IF I can't find anyone else?" " I want to date other guys, but WHAT IF he dates other girls?" These questions invite curiosity, which then turns into complacency. "I'll just stay and deal with it." Instead of taking the risk of change, we try to make things work when we already know the person won't change for the better. Allowing "replacers" in my life put me in a place of fear because I was too emotionally invested in wanting to start over.

Moments when I was at my lowest, I would gaze away and think about my relationship decisions. "Would things have been different if I knew my father? Would that have helped my choices? Would I have been aware of my self worth because he was in my life to guide me?" For me, I realize now these questions might be a little irrelevant because my testimony has already been written, and God has graced me through all of my foolish past mistakes. But still, I wonder…what if?

Strong father figures give off a sense of protection and security. It's always depicted that when a girl is old enough to start dating, her father feels like it's his fatherly right to put a sense of fear in her date. Why? I've always believed this was done so that the guy would understand that the girl he's dating is being held to high regard. But I also believe this wasn't just for the date. Girls get a sense of how valued and precious we are to our fathers in those moments. Daughters should appreciate their fathers placing them on a pedestal because it sets the tone for self-respect and knowing your worth. I know some fathers can be a bit over the top, but looking back on what I've never had, it saddens me when other girls don't appreciate what they do have. Can fathers be over the edge? Oh! Absolutely! But for those of you reading this who have had the privilege of your father(s) being that protective hedge over your life, please be appreciative. What we don't realize is that fathers coming on so strong sets a level of expectation for that 'young man' (as my mother would call him) to not cross any lines without an invitation. It gives guys a level of expectations that he needs to uphold and a standard he needs to meet if he wants to continue to court you.

Even though my father wasn't around, one of the many things I loved about my mother is that she would come off just as intimidating as a father would. My stepfather had always been pretty laid back, so as long as everything 'seemed' good, he was okay with it. My mother, not so much. My mother made sure that it was known that I was a gem in her eyes. I remember dating guys in high school and my mother would drill them up on everything! Looking back in retrospect, having my mother so active in my high school years with my teachers, friends, and their parents was truly a bonus!. Because of my mother's relationship with mostly everyone at school, she knew all about anybody who showed interest in me, and they knew all about her. My mom was never unfair, but she did evaluate where the "potential boyfriend" hung around, whom he hung around, and his reputation at school. Even though I was and will always be appreciative of my mother's protective nature, there's nothing like a girl having a father around to set that standard for dating.

REPLACERS

Are there any married women reading this book? Do you feel like maybe there's a possibility that your spouse is or was a "replacer?" Well, I can tell you first hand that I believe that possibility is very high for most of us. I can't say that I honestly tried to make my spouse a 'replacer.' I just happened to be in a place of confronting my inner feelings about my natural father when we met.

When I first met my husband, I was still dealing with some emotional issues. A few years prior, I had just gotten out of a pretty serious relationship. Even while we were dating, I always kind of knew that my husband would end up being the guy I married. The more time we spent courting, the more I felt (even early on) that my dating days were starting to come to an end. Side note: For all my single ladies, when you FINALLY meet 'him' you'll know. Trust me on this. So with this in mind, I allowed my husband (then boyfriend) to become closer to me than any other man I had ever dated. I introduced a vulnerable side of myself to him that, to my surprise, he found very beautiful. I introduced him to the broken version of me. I wanted him to see that outside of the woman he thought was so well put together, there was a deeper root to me that stemmed back 30 years ago. I wanted my husband to understand that if I tested his patience, I was just seeing if he really loved me enough to stick around. If I pushed him away, just to run back to him again, it was to satisfy this desire of control since I had issues of abandonment. If I came across extra needy, it was because I never had the influence of my natural father around to settle those emotions. If I had issues submitting to him, it was because I needed my father to teach me how to let him lead. Needless to say, my husband is still hanging in there with me during this process. I know there have been plenty of days he may have thought I was a basket case, but I'm thankful he recognized that I was trying to purge through my emotions so that I could overcome them. And that's what this is all about ladies…overcoming! No one ever said that we had to submit ourselves to the brokenness and pain that our absentee fathers left. The best method I've discovered thus far is identifying the hurt, getting rid of the replacers, and finding a release. A release can be found in therapy, crying it out, talking it out, praying, fasting, meditating, or like me…writing about it!

REPLACERS

Replacers are not just guys! I have heard the testimonies of deeply hurt women that have dealt with abandonment issues and have discovered that they replaced their hurt by coping in other ways. This can be drinking, turning to drugs, being confrontational (as a defense mechanism), promiscuity, and remorsefully for some, attempted suicide. Some of you have actually ran from relationships due to the fear of loving a man. This is not uncommon. The misconception is that ALL women with 'daddy issues' gravitate to men, when in fact, a lot of women with 'daddy issues' tend to go the opposite direction from affection. Hence turning to substance abuse, having a bitter heart, or even trying to end their lives. Some of you that are in this position feel that if you protect yourself, then you don't have to deal with the possibility of rejection. Rejection in life comes in many forms, but the key is how you deal with the hurt, not how you can run from the hurt.

Have you ever heard "Beauty for Ashes" by Tye Tribbett? If not, take a listen. The song implies how we present God with our ashes (problems) and he trades them for beauty. Who wouldn't serve an amazing God like this? What am I saying to you? As you journey through healing, release your problems to God. One thing I do know for sure is that God is a God of plot twists. He loves to turn our stories into beautiful testaments of his love and delivering power.

LET US BE GRATEFUL TO THE MIRROR FOR REVEALING TO US OUR APPEARANCE ONLY.

-SAMUEL BUTLER

chapter eight

MIRROR, MIRROR ON THE WALL

Often, we don't appreciate the value of a mirror. We underestimate its power to help us see what we present to others daily. Every day, we take a glance in the mirror or walk right past it. But what if there were no more mirrors? What if every mirror completely vanished? What would you do? Sometimes, it's not until something is unavailable that we recognize its value.

Mirrors allow us to see the version of us that everyone sees. They provide us with the opportunity to adjust anything that might be out of place. Personally, I love a good visit to the mirror. Anytime I walk past one, I check my clothes for neatness, ensure my hair is straight, and make sure nothing is in my teeth. Like many, I want to make sure that I'm always presentable.

One day, as I was doing a check in the mirror, a thought occurred to me. "Malika, have you considered how what's within you is reflecting outwardly? How do you "look" beyond what the mirror can see?" I began to think, "Is there a mirror that can help us see inwardly? Is there a mirror that can reveal the baggage we're carrying or the pain we're projecting onto others?" Yes. There is. It's called accountability.

Accountability is rarely used, but it holds so much power. Have you ever been around someone who always blamed his or her current behavior on past disappointments? I mean, they constantly blame everyone else in their life for not being where they want to be. It can be overwhelming to talk to someone like that, and it requires a lot of patience! These conversations are especially frustrating when you can see that the individual has so much potential to be great — if they would get out of their own way.

We've all heard stories about people who had a traumatic start in life, and instead of letting it define the rest of their life, they learned from their mistakes and turned things around. We admire these individuals because they took the opposition and their disadvantages and made something incredible out of their lives. However, we must be careful not to write off those who haven't come to this place in life. If we are honest, we haven't always been there. I know I wasn't. We've all had moments of doubt and weakness, and many of us are still there right now. So let's have this conversation about accountability.

I can recall times when I felt so defeated due to my abandonment issues. The thought of being delivered and walking in my purpose seemed more like a fairy tale than a reality. For years, I believed that every unfair, painful, degrading, and even life-threatening moment that happened to me was due to my father's abandonment. One day, it hit me that everything wasn't his fault. Blaming him only robbed me of the chance to turn my life around. I arrived at this place by taking accountability for the things I could change. There is absolutely nothing I could have done differently on September 22, 1987. There was nothing I could say to make my father stay. There is nothing I can do to make him reach out and be a part of my life. I can't make him see that he has a responsibility as my father. However, I can choose to heal. I can choose to check my heart and be honest with how I feel. I can choose to lean on God and allow him to fill the void in my life. I can't go back and fix the things I did out of hurt, rejection, abandonment, and pain, but I can make better decisions moving forward.

Many of you reading this book may feel like there is something you could have done to change the circumstances you were born in. Regretfully, I hate to inform you, but there is nothing different you could have done about what card life dealt you. Fortunately, there is something significant you can do now -- hold yourself accountable for your future.

Just to be clear, accountability is not just the act of taking ownership of a wrongdoing or blaming self. It's accepting what you can't change and acknowledging what you can change. Holding yourself accountable opens the door of growth and allows you to see where you need to mature. It frees you from carrying the weight of being a victim and allows you the freedom to make future wiser decisions. Accountability is our personal internal mirror. It allows us to see what's been done to us, but also what we can do for ourselves.

GET YOUR HEAD IN THE GAME

I've been in some pretty rough seasons that seemed never-ending! I'm sure we can all relate. I so desperately wanted God to deliver from those seasons, but I didn't realize that most of what I was battling was all in my mind. My mind told me that I would never be free from my distress and that my issues of insecurity and abandonment would always be with me.

Have you ever heard of the expression, "Mind over matter?" Our minds have the ability and intelligence capacity to overcome whatever the body may be physically going through.

Growing up in NY, I loved to ride my bike around my old neighborhood. Riding a bike often comes with many cuts, scrapes, and bruises. Ouch! There were times when I hurt myself so badly that my mom would run to the scene of the incident with alcohol, gauze pads, and band-aids (as if I wasn't already embarrassed enough about falling off my bike) and she would apply the alcohol directly to the cut. I hated this. To take my mind off the sting of the alcohol, she would distract me. Sometimes, I wouldn't even feel the alcohol being applied to my cut. This is just how powerful our minds are.

If we are going to heal properly, we must recognize the

power of our minds because that's where change begins. I've stayed in trials that should have been temporary simply because my mind hadn't been fully delivered. Now, I'm learning how to walk in the freedom that God has granted me. His plan is never for us to be in bondage after He's broken the bondage chains in our lives. We just have to comprehend this in our minds so that our bodies, hearts, and actions can follow.

You, reader, have a purpose. Regardless of the father that walked away from you or the broken relationship you had or still have, you have a purpose. To walk into that purpose, you must become acquainted with accountability and honesty.

I know this can be difficult. I don't write this book as some sort of fearless gladiator. For me, it wasn't easy to look back at my own 'behavioral reflection' and see what I was doing. I made excuses for every poor choice I made in life, especially in my relationships. I remember being in a verbally abusive relationship some years back. People in my life asked me, "Why are you still dealing with him and all of his issues?" But in typical "Malika" fashion, I always gave some creative excuse about why I chose to stay. Until one day, I realized that I couldn't continue to make excuses for someone who continually tried to tear me down. It started with me choosing to look in the mirror and look at what I was reflecting back to myself. All I could see in my reflection was a cycle of bad choices.

What I found more astonishing is that I began to thank

God for what He was allowing me to see. If you don't ever see your flaws, how will you know what needs to be corrected? The more I stayed before the Lord in prayer, He helped me to see what I needed help with and slowly but surely helped me to break cycles in my life. But this part was not easy! The Lord charged me (just like I'm charging you) to look deep inside and take ownership of issues that I've allowed to paralyze me from being at my best.

As you begin the journey of self-reflection, know that the mirror is not a boxing ring. It's not you versus you. It's not you versus who hurt you. The mirror of accountability is not where you should see yourself as a failure. It's an intimate setting where you can be as open as you want to be. You can look at yourself and come to terms with what you've allowed in your life, what you're ashamed of, and even what you want to change. Will there be tears? Yes. But speaking words of affirmation will continue to build your character and protect your self-esteem. Here are a few other key points I want you to remember as you prepare to look in your internal mirror.

- Submit yourself to God in all you do, think, and believe
- Acknowledge the hurt and pain
- Realize the abandonment had NOTHING to do with you!
- Acknowledge the decisions you've made (This is accountability)

- Remember that YOU dictate your future and its success (God gives us the privilege of choice)
- Forgive yourself (No exceptions to this)
- Speak words of affirmation and encouragement
- Walk in purpose and make no apologies for it
- Realize the power in your reflection!

HE BROUGHT ME UP ALSO OUT OF A HORRIBLE PIT, OUT OF THE MIRY CLAY, AND SET MY FEET UPON A ROCK AND ESTABLISHED MY GOINGS.

-PSALM 40

chapter nine

FINDING MYSELF

2008 and 2009 were the most challenging two years of my life. I struggled with my identity and didn't have a clue who I was as a person. I wondered if "finding myself" was something I was capable of doing. It was hard hearing people advise me, "Find yourself. Find out who you are what you like." I didn't even know where to begin. This was the right advice, but without direction or practicality on how to follow through, it was pointless. My extreme clinginess in relationships was, of course, a result of fatherlessness, but there was more. I clung so tightly because I had no idea who I was. It was like my only definition or identity was what I was to them. And I couldn't let that go. I knew who I wanted to be. Often, I had visions of who and what God wanted me to become. Unfortunately, I couldn't get out of my own way. I felt so lost.

In one relationship, in particular, I was completely consumed with the person I was dating. He was all I thought about. I adjusted my plans to be with him. Our relationship was on my mind morning, noon, and night. I began to change everything about me, what I liked, where I liked to go, and even my taste in music. I became ignorant of my desires and had no sense of self-identity. All I knew was that I was in a relationship, and the rest would figure itself out.

One day, that man looked me in my eyes and said, "I need you to find a life of your own. What do you like to do?"

This devastated me, but I knew he was right. Besides working most of the time, I would just come home and wait for 'further instruction' on what moves we were making that night or the upcoming weekend. Even though he was right, I needed a life, and I needed one fast, I still had no clue where to start. His statement, however, jolted something in me and made me aware of the change I needed to make.

Shortly after this, a coworker and I became really good friends and began to hang out frequently after work. This became my new norm. I spent less time at home because I was out enjoying the newfound life my boyfriend so desperately wanted me to find. I met new people, enjoyed different conversations, and experienced everything I thought I needed from my boyfriend at that time.

Gratefully, this friendship with my coworker didn't only lead me to fun and meeting new people. It also led me to Christ. It was in our connection that I became more familiar with God's plan of salvation and began to walk as the woman God designed me to be all along. It was like

God removed the blindfold from my eyes and allowed me to see the new person that I was becoming. Naturally, the boyfriend who encouraged me to go 'find myself' wasn't too thrilled when I wasn't home as often. But I didn't care! As hurtful as it was to hear him say those words to me about my life, it needed to be said. Sometimes the hurtful words of others are just the fuel you need to head in the right direction!

It's not so easy to break away from an 'identity crisis' issue and go 'find yourself.' Some of you are either walking into this season in of your life or trying to figure out how to come out of it. Know that the process may be filled with lowliness and loneliness. It takes time to disconnect from someone who has basically been programming your days for you. You may feel helpless and unable to find enough power to love yourself. Even though your friends may care, there will be times when it doesn't seem like they understand. Yes, anyone can say, "Girl, forget him! Go find who you are!" However, during these times, you need someone to show you how to do that. It's okay if you choose to distance yourself from those who give you advice without substance.

There will be moments when you'll want to beat yourself up for ever getting into these situations. You cry, "Why am I like this? When will I find me? When will I be happy with my own company?" At those moments, understand that what you are dealing with is not uncommon. Most people who have been abandoned by their fathers feel the need to 'latch' onto men. Though many women won't admit it, it's possible to battle with clinginess in relationships, especially when we have daddy issues. We see them as our only 'male constant,' and we begin to absorb everything about them, i.e., habits, hobbies, attitude, etc. It is very easy to lose yourself in this process, especially if you' deal with the fear of losing another male figure. You want to learn and know everything about them even so much so that you're willing to lose yourself in the process. However, just like we discussed in the previous chapter, don't spend time beating yourself up for how you got there. Make a plan to uncover your identity and move forward. I don't have all the answers, but on the next few pages, I want to share my journey with you, and I pray that it will help you along your own.

JUST ME & GOD

I've seen so many women conquer this process in their lives without a care in the world. I would often look at them and wonder, "How do you do that? How do you not care about men being in your life? Where did you get that kind of confidence?" My biggest issue with 'finding myself' was that I lacked confidence. I wasn't bold enough to have the mindset that I didn't care if I was with someone or not. I couldn't even lie to myself like it didn't matter. It did matter to me — a lot! Being with somebody made me feel like somebody. Because I wasn't confident enough in who I was as a woman, I became what he liked. My whole being became about him because I didn't want to lose him. Did I know better? Yes. On the inside, I was actually ashamed. I knew better, but I didn't want to do better.

After my coworker turned friend introduced me to the Lord, things began to change. I thought about all I'd been through with men in my life… my father's absence …this boyfriend's mistreatment of me… that boyfriend's disregard of my feelings etc. I became mentally exhausted. I realized that I'd spent so much of my life hurt about men, and I never took time out for myself. I got back into school and became active within my church. Day by day, I started discovering who I was and what I liked. I even began to change what I tolerated. Did I still feel lonely at times? Of course. When I wasn't confident in my ability to continue along my process, I put my confidence in God. He helped me cope with going to bed alone. I began to say no more and walked within the authority that God had given to me. If I needed to cry, I cried. If I needed to talk to someone, the Lord provided a support system of caring women that I could trust. If I needed a late night vent session, I prayed and poured my heart out at God's feet. When the feeling for companionship started to overwhelm me, I asked the Lord to fill that void until the time was right for me to marry. As the days went on, I began to find the joy inside of me, and I loved it!

Trying to find out who you are without the distraction of a man while dealing with your desire for a companion is tough. One thing that helped me was remembering that feelings are temporary decisions that can cause permanent damage. I implore you not to get distracted by something temporary. The season of 'finding yourself' isn't designed to be easy. It's built to show your strength and character. It's meant to define your inner ability to push past distractions and traps. But most importantly, it's meant to escort you into your purpose!

It may feel like you'll never discover who you are, but finding yourself is possible! There are no secret combinations of actions you must take. You only need to put effort into it. Like many other important decisions in life, it starts with a choice. You have to chose to explore who you are and allow God to lead the way. Before we get into the final chapter, let me share something that a lot of married people won't tell you. Even as a wife, I am still discovering who I am, whose I am (which is most important), and what I like to do. Yep, you guessed it! The process of finding yourself never ends. It's not a destination. It's a journey. At every pit stop, you'll find yourself taking off more of what you thought you needed, putting on more of what you do need, learning things about yourself, and loving who you are becoming. Here are a few things I did on my journey to discovering myself.

MAKE AN EFFORT

Every day, I searched for joy as I discovered who I was. I booked day trips to New York (or any other place I could afford) just to spend some time alone. This made me happy. Figure out what brings you joy and make an effort to do it. Don't feel selfish about taking the time to invest in yourself. If you like to travel, shop, read, or even want to further your education, make an effort to start the process.

YIELD

In some cases, we believe it's possible to overcome our circumstances without God's help. God wants to be involved in EVERY aspect of our lives. He's a concerned and

loving God who wants to be apart of your growing process. He has so much that He wants to do through you, but you'll never discover your true purpose without yielding to his will...and his assistance.

BE CONTENT

If you aren't married, appreciate this time to discover yourself in your singleness. Realize that God is giving you this time (like He did for me) to grow and heal. Trust me! There is someone out there waiting on you. But for now, remember that 'finding yourself' is your 'selfish time.' This time is designed for you to rediscover who you are and what you're aiming to be.

GET OUT OF YOUR OWN WAY

Some of the situations we have dealt with are because we stood in our way of growth. It seems so much easier to just resort back to what we already know to do versus aiming to do what's best for us. Finding yourself isn't comfortable, but you must press through. Often, comfort doesn't produce the necessary results. Know that there is purpose in your pain, sacrifice, and even self-denial. Get out of your way and see all that you can become.

STAY FOCUSED

Sometimes we are our biggest distraction. We seem to dwell so much on the past that it hinders us from staying focused on what's ahead. Eyes forward, soldier!

Due to your abandonment issues, finding yourself is necessary. It's the key to recognizing your value beyond the part of your DNA that you know little about. Maybe you never had the privilege of getting to know your father or being influenced by him. It's okay to be disappointed about this, but don't allow it to make you neglect to learn about yourself. Finding yourself won't change the past, but it will help you accept the things you may never know or even understand. You owe it to yourself to keep going in discovering who you are despite your past.

FORGIVENESS ISN'T APPROVING WHAT
HAPPENED, IT'S CHOOSING TO RISE ABOVE IT.

-ROBIN SHARMA

chapter ten

HEALING.
GROWING. FORGIVING.

O nce I got older, I had more in-depth conversations with my mother about my biological father. In one of our discussions, she confessed something that took me a while to swallow. My father held me once. All my life, I'd thought he'd never even seen me as a child. My mother told me that not only had he seen me, but he held me in his arms. He even said that I was a beautiful baby, but I just wasn't....well...his.

As I thought about what she shared, I couldn't help but feel angry. How could he have held me and felt absolutely no connection? He didn't even take the time to consider the possibility that he was my father. It would be one thing if he left when my mother announced her pregnancy and was never seen or heard from again. However, there is another feeling that comes over you when you know the man who abandoned you actually held you in his arms and still didn't chose to be in your life. No compassion.

No second-guessing of his decision. Nothing. It seems so cold, cynical, and insensitive that he could actually look at me, hold me, see me as a defenseless newborn, and never take the time to confirm his paternity. Over the years, I accepted my past and learned to embrace my present. I'm alive and well despite "dad" not wanting me. Nothing can defeat God's plan for my life. Nothing is going to stop me from getting what God has for me.

One of my favorite inspirational songs is 'Imagine Me' by Kirk Franklin. Yes, another song that I highly recommend you listen to! The song is about imagining yourself being free from everything that seems to hold you back from being at your best and being free. A lyric in the song states, "Healed from what my daddy did…" When I heard this, I would tear up because I could see myself coming out of the mental prison I'd put myself in. I would feel this overwhelming feeling of forgiveness, healing, and even deliverance all at once. I realized being free was something I didn't have to imagine anymore… I was free!

I was beginning to walk and even think as a woman who no longer allowed her past abandonment to keep her from living her best life. Yes, Me! The woman who dealt with abandonment as a little girl, feeling insecure and unwanted. Yes, Me! The woman who grew up hiding her insecurities because she didn't want to let on that she was hurting. Yes, Me! The woman who didn't know how to cope with her father being absent, so she envied other women who had real 'father-daughter' relationships. Yes,

Me! The woman who didn't know what true love was from a man, so she began looking for it in all the wrong places. Yes, Me! The woman who was so dependent on male companionship that she lost herself and who she wanted to be.

Now, insert yourself into those statements. Consider your past, consider your pain, consider what you've allowed, and even what you blocked.

You've faced so much, and you didn't allow it to consume you. Now, imagine discovering who you want to be outside of your pain. Just like the song says in a particular verse, "Imagine me, being free, trusting you totally." Realize that you no longer have to imagine. You can just be! Isn't it beautiful to know that you hold all the cards when it comes to being free from whatever is holding you down?

It took me a while to see the beauty in coming out of my mental bondage because I was so comfortable there. I was comfortable in my poor decision-making and low self-esteem. Why? Because it didn't challenge me to be better, it didn't cause me to step outside of myself and push myself forward. I didn't like the 'unfamiliar' (especially if it challenged me), so I stayed within my 'bondage bubble' and allowed my 'daddy issues' to make decisions for me my entire life.

GROWING

One thing I admire about my past is that it allowed me to see just how sovereign God is. Psalms 40:2 says, "He brought me up also out a horrible pit, out of the miry clay, and set my feet upon a rock, and established my goings." A friend of mines once told me that the Lord has the power to push 'reset' on your life. He can reset your way of thinking and will help you move in the right direction. That's exactly what He's done for me.

The Lord groomed my way of thinking so that I could grow past my hurt. I began to let go of the hatred in my heart for my father and replace it with more compassion. I realized that, just like me, he is a living soul that God cares very much for.

No, nothing can excuse the poor choice he made to abandon his responsibility, but it's not my place to choose his fate. I had to grow past the hatred that had sprouted up in my heart. My life could have been infested with hate and unforgiveness if I had allowed those feelings to take control.

Trust me. I've had my time to be angry, cry, and even loathe his very existence. But when the opportunity to grow and let go of my pain presented itself, it was an offer I couldn't refuse. Don't get me wrong. I contended with God and told him that I was entitled to be upset for however long I chose. I figured that since I was the offended and not the offender, it wasn't my place to do any work on myself. It was his problem -- not mine. God didn't fight me on the issue. He just revealed to me how much freedom I was robbing myself of. He showed me that self-growth would lead me to another way of thinking that could free me. He told me that if I was able to push myself to grow past all the hurt and walk away from this disappointment, I could finally spend the rest of my life focusing on what's important, which is myself.

In order to accept God's opportunity to grow, you must find yourself valuable enough to invest in. You are a whole person outside of the disappointments you have faced with your father or anyone else who has let you down in life. Take the necessary time to invest in yourself to replenish all the years you spent in pain due to disappointments. Your outlook on life will begin to change drastically if you choose to grow beyond what you feel.

FORGIVING

After I allowed the Lord to reset my thinking, I felt a change in how I felt toward my father. This is where forgiveness comes in. I'm almost certain that you've heard the saying, "Forgiveness is for you, not the other person," at least a million times! But this is not just a saying, it's true! Forgiveness frees you from feeling tied down emotionally. It sets you free to live the life you desire. Even though forgiving a father for abandoning or not making the best attempt to have a relationship with you is not easy, it is imperative in order for you to move on.

Think about this... If you were a prisoner serving time for a crime you were wrongfully accused of, what would you do if the opportunity to walk free from prison was presented to you? I'm pretty sure you would dash towards the nearest exit! I doubt your response would be, "No, I just can't seem to move past the wrongful conviction in my mind and how no one believed me. So I'd rather stay." Would you really sacrifice your freedom because you just can't seem to move past what was done to you? Well, refusing to forgive is choosing to do exactly that.

You don't have to stay within the confinements of hurt and abuse. You are being given the opportunity to 'walk free' from the inner prison sentence that's keeping you mentally bound. The bottom line is, you have to forgive!

You might be thinking, "Do I forgive a man who left me in such a tormented state? Do I forgive a father who doesn't want to spend any time with me? Do I forgive a man who doesn't see me as special to him?" The answer is, yes. You have to forgive. Why? It's simple… it unlocks the door to your freedom.

The freedom that I'm speaking of is your freedom to love again. Mother Theresa said it best, "If we really want to love, we must learn how to forgive." The expression, "Hurt people, hurt people," exposes how most of us choose to live our lives after disappointment. We most often choose to cling to the hurt as a cover-up for our avoidance to heal. So what happens? We lash out on those who had nothing to do with the pain. For women like us dealing with abandonment or daddy issues, we tend to take our issues out on the next person in line. This tends to be our spouses or even potential spouses.

This is why I am a firm believer that forgiveness is such

an essential key in unlocking all that life has in store for you. If I were to have allowed the abandonment issues I've dealt with to overcome my decision making any further, it would have divided me from what God had intended for me to receive. So many of you may be forfeiting a beautiful future because of an unfortunate past.

#LIVINGMYBESTLIFE

It was never God's intention for any of us to go throughout life defeated and broken. Consider this. The Bible says in John 10:10, "I come that you might have life and that more abundantly." To receive the abundance, we have to push past the pain. God is not oblivious to the inner hurt you may be feeling. There is absolutely nothing that escapes Him. Furthermore, He is not allowing what you've faced in life to dictate the plans that He has in store for you. Why should you? Don't forfeit your future.

On social media, people often use the hashtag #livingmybestlife. I never quite got what that meant. Most of the time, the people who I saw using it were referring to a pretty background behind them with clear blue water and palm trees, or some sort of famous landmark that tells you they're on a well-spent vacation. I also saw people use this when they wanted to showcase a picture of them going out for a night of fun or achieving some great accomplishment. While there's nothing wrong with this, I often wondered, "Are they really living their best lives?"

Since its evolution, social media has been known to

be the biggest platform for "fantasy lives" that has ever existed. These are lives people want you to believe they're living. In reality, there's a lot more going on then what we can see. How do I know? Well, I was masking my pain and reality way before it became popular on social media. Most of my early life was one big fake #livingmybestlife hashtag. Having daddy issues has a way of teaching you how to perfect this.

Am I saying that everyone who uses this hashtag is covering up something? Absolutely not. Some people may actually be experiencing what they perceive to be the best version of their lives. However, considering that we are now living in a generation full of fake facades and masks, it is safe to say that some are hiding behind pain that they don't want the world privy to.

We all deserve to live our best life. What that may look like for you will be different for the next person. Nevertheless, the prerequisite to living your best life is cleaning the inside. You can take as many vacations as your heart desires, fly to the farthest destination on the planet, but if you are carrying inner baggage, the weight of your problems will always be with you.

There is so much more life out there for you to live! Your name is on it. It's called "Your life." You are not your father's mistake, and you are definitely bigger than the daddy issues you have struggled with. You are more than your past mistakes and hurt. You are an evolving testament of God's love and keeping power. Living your best life starts with you breaking free from the shell of who you used to be.

After reading this book, know that you are officially on your journey of healing and restoration. You have the tools you need, and most importantly, you have your God to guide you. What are you waiting for? Go forward and live your #bestlife!

ACKNOWLEDGMENTS

As I wrote this book, I often thought of whom I wanted to dedicate this book to. I felt that a book's dedication should acknowledge someone in particular who provided influence and inspiration for this book. As I thought about it, there's not just one person who made this book possible. So, I would like to take this time to acknowledge the persons in my life who have been pillars of strength and inspiration. To my wonderful husband, Ezekiel, you have been a source of strength and accountability since this process began. As my husband, you were first in knowing about this journey that I decided to embark on. Did you ever think that this day would come? Ah! Of course, you did! That is because you see nothing but greatness in me. When it pertains to me, you tolerate nothing less than exceptional because that is all you've ever seen in me. You've encouraged my obedience to the Lord's call and held me accountable for every moment I spent writing this book or shamefully, sometimes the lack thereof. You gave me the foresight to see what this book could become and the influence it would have to encourage those fighting similar battles as mine. I share with you every page in this book.

To my remarkable mother, I would truly be remiss if I didn't take the time to express my gratitude towards you. From the beginning, you were present. From the beginning, you were my support. From the beginning, you were my inspiration and example of how to move forward despite life's challenges. It was unfortunate that life handed you a cup of pain so early. I imagine that being a single mother, young, and still trying to figure out life for yourself was no easy task, but, in typical 'mom' fashion, you handled every hard moment with grace. This acknowledgment can in no way repay what you've done for me over the years, especially how you protected me from the pain of an absentee father, but hopefully, it shows the world a snippet of what I know to be true. That you're amazing!

Lastly, to my readers, I dedicate every page towards your healing process. Through obedience to God, I was able to write a book that I hope you find helpful in knowing that healing, growing, and forgiving is possible. Your latter will be greater!

ABOUT THE AUTHOR

malika Roebuck was born September 22, 1987 in Brooklyn New York. As a New York native, she finds irony in how much she deeply enjoys quiet places and serenity. Despite Malika's early start in life having dealt with an abandoned father, she was determined from an early age to turn her story of emotional affliction due to her 'Daddy issues' into a pillar of hope for other young women that can relate to her story. Throughout Malika's life, God has favored her in spite of the broken pieces life has tried to hand her early on.

She is married to the love of her life, Ezekiel Roebuck, and is approaching the completion of her Marketing Degree at the University of Maryland. As a first time author, "Daddy's Girl" is a huge milestone in her life that will prayerfully inspire and uplift the lives of many. Through her obeisance to God's instructions to write her story, "Daddy's Girl" will prayerfully inspire you to heal your past, grow beyond your pain and forgive the ones that have hurt you.

STAY CONNECTED

Thank you for reading, *Daddy's Girl*. Malika looks forward to connecting with you and keeping you updated on her next releases. Below are a few ways you can connect with the author.

FACEBOOK Daddy's Girl
INSTAGRAM @book_daddysgirl/missglo2mrsroe
EMAIL daddysgirlthebook@gmail.com
WEBSITE www.malikadroebuck.com

Made in the USA
Middletown, DE
06 September 2020